THE TVP® COOKBOOK

Burgers Burritos Spaghetti Balls

Red Chili

Fajit Stir Fry

Red Beans & Rice Sauerbraten

Burritos Spaghetti Balls

Burgers Burritos Spaghetti Balls

Chunks in Creole Sauce Tamale Pie

by Dorothy R. Bates

Chinese Barbecued Chunks Gyros

Empanadas Lasagne Stroganoff

Burgers Burritos Spaghetti Balls

Red Pepper Stir Fry Curries Chili

The Book Publishing Company
Summertown, TN 38483

Cover and interior design: Barbara McNew
Cover photos: Thomas Johns
Illustrations: Esther Traugot

On the front cover: Red Pepper Stir-Fry, page 86

On the back cover, clockwise from upper left: Spaghetti Sauce with Italian Spaghetti Balls, pages 56 and 57, Country Chili, page 22, and Chinese Barbecued Chunks, page 13.

TVP ® is a registered trademark of the Archer Daniels Midland Company Decatur, Illinois

Library of Congress
Cataloging-in-Publication Information

Bates, Dorothy R.
    The TVP®cookbook / by Dorothy R. Bates.
        p. cm.
    Includes index
    ISBN 0-913990-79-5
    1. Cookery (Textured soy proteins) I. Title.
    TX814.5.T48B37   1991
    6416'5655- -dc20   91-27400
                                                       CIP

ISBN 0-913990-79-5

03 02 01 00 13 12 11 10

Calculations for the nutritional analyses in this book are based on the average number of servings listed with the recipes and the average amount of an ingredient if a range is called for. Calculations are rounded up to the nearest gram. If two options for an ingredient are listed, the first one is used. Not included are fat used for frying, unless the amount is specified in the recipe, optional ingredients, or serving suggestions.

The Book Publishing Company
P.O. Box 99
Summertown, TN 38483
1-888-260-8458

Table of Contents

Introduction

TVP ® stands for texturized vegetable protein, a food product made from soybeans. The initials are the registered trademark of the *Archer Daniels Midland Company* of Decatur, Illinois, who has been manufacturing it for more than 20 years. Ninety per cent of **TVP** ® is used in packaged or canned foods; if you read labels, you'll see "textured soy flour" listed as an ingredient. **TVP** ® is produced from soy flour after the soybean oil has been extracted, then cooked under pressure, extruded and dried.

TVP ® comes in several sizes, from small granules or flakes to chunks and slices 1 to 2 inches long. It is a staple food in the cupboards of most vegetarian cooks. The small granules or flakes and the larger chunky pieces or slices can be used in a variety of recipes to add texture, fiber and protein to meals. If you can't find these varieties of **TVP** ® in your health food store, you can obtain them from the mail order source on page 95.

Nutrition

TVP ® has zero cholesterol. It can be fortified with vitamins, including Vitamin B12. An excellent source of protein and fiber, **TVP** ® is low in sodium and has almost no fat. It is high in potassium, is a good source of the essential amino acids and also contributes calcium and magnesium to one's diet. **TVP** ® adds character but not calories to many meal time favorites.

Reconstituting

The small granules are very quick to reconstitute, or can be added dry to soups and sauces. The larger chunks are more tender if presoaked and simmered in moisture. Microwave ovens are a timesaver. You can prepare a double batch of chunks, enough for 2 or 3 recipes, and the cooked **TVP** ® will keep in the refrigerator several days. Or freeze some to thaw later in a microwave or in the refrigerator. Once **TVP** ® has been rehydrated, it must be kept under refrigeration.

How to Use TVP®

To rehydrate the small granules, pour 7/8 cup boiling water over 1 cup **TVP®**. Stir and let stand for 5 to 10 minutes.

For chunk-sized TVP® or the slices: pour 1 cup boiling water over 1 cup chunky **TVP®**. Stir, cover the pan and let soak for 5 minutes. I've found that adding 1 Tbsp. ketchup or a mild vinegar to the hot water promotes absorption. If cooking on top of stove, add another cup of liquid, bring chunks and liquid to a boil, reduce heat and simmer for 15-20 minutes until chunks are fork tender but not mushy. Vegetable broth or stock can be used for the liquid. **To cook in a microwave**, cover tightly with plastic wrap and cook on high for 5-6 minutes; check after 2 minutes and add a little more liquid if needed.

Using Your Microwave

We used a microwave oven rated at 700 watts at high power with cavity dimensions of 10 3/4 (H) x 16 3/8 (W) x 13 3/8 (D). Because microwave ovens vary in power and size, follow the instructions that accompany your own oven and increase or decrease cooking times as needed.

The following symbol will indicate recipes that can be made in your microwave:

Nutritional Information for TVP®

Granules
(per 1/4 cup dry - 21 gm.)
Calories: 59
Protein: 11 gm.
Carbohydrates: 7 gm.
Fat: .2 gm.

Flakes and Chunks
(per 1/4 cup dry - 14 gm.)
Calories: 39
Protein: 7 gm.
Carbohydrates: 4 gm.
Fat: .1 gm.

Vitamins and Minerals (mg per 100 gm of TVP®)

Biotin: .07
Calcium: 340
Copper: 1.3
Folic acid: .35
Iron: 8
Magnesium: 347
Manganese: 2.6
Niacin: 3.00
Pantothenic acid: 1.30

Phosphorus: 700
Potassium: 2200
Riboflavin: .33
Sodium: 15
Thiamine: .60
Vitamin B6: .5
Vitamin B12: trace
Zinc: 5.5

INGREDIENTS

Five Spice Powder

Five spice powder can be obtained in oriental or health food stores, or can be made by combining 1 tsp. ground fennel, 1 tsp cinnamon, 1/2 tsp. ground star anise, 1/2 tsp. ground cloves and 1/4 tsp. Szechuan or cayenne pepper.

Instant Gluten Flour

Instant gluten flour or vital wheat gluten is different from the high gluten wheat flour used for bread baking. Vital wheat gluten is actually pulverized dried gluten made from wheat flour after all the starch has been removed. Adding water to it immediately reconstitutes it into raw gluten. It is available in some health food stores or from mail order sources listed on page 95.

Mirin

Mirin is a slightly sweet, lightly fermented liquid made from rice. It is delicious in oriental flavored sauces and marinades.

Nutritional Yeast

We use Saccharomyces cerevisiae, golden flakes of a yeast grown on a molasses base. Its flavor has been called cheesey and nutty. It is an excellent source of the B vitamins, especially riboflavin, and is 40% protein. Do not use brewers or other yeasts in these recipes. Nutritional yeast is available at health food stores, usually in both flakes and powder form. If you use powder, reduce the amount in these recipes by half. It is available in some health food stores or from mail order sources listed on page 95.

Shiitake Mushrooms

To use dried shiitake mushrooms, place in a bowl and cover with hot water: mushroom stems are usually cut off and discarded. Let stand at least 15 minutes. Lift out the mushrooms, being careful to avoid the sand in the bottom of the dish. Some of the soaking liquid can be used in stock if carefully decanted or strained through a damp cloth to avoid sediment.

Ingredients, *continued on next page*

Shoyu and Tamari

Both shoyu and tamari are forms of soy sauce made the natural, time consuming way by cleaning, cooking, mashing, and fermenting soybeans over a long period of time, then filtering and pasteurizing the sauce. Tamari is usually made solely from soybeans, while shoyu may contain wheat. In the natural fermenting process salt water is used and lends the salty flavor to shoyu and tamari, but these natural products contain far less sodium than ordinary table salt. Much soy sauce sold in supermarkets is chemically fermented in a matter of hours and has caramel coloring and salt added. We recommend using either shoyu or tamari for the best results in these recipes.

Vegetable Stock or Broth

This broth can be made by cooking coarsely chopped vegetables (onions, carrots, garlic, potatoes, and turnips, for example) with enough water to cover them about 2 inches. Add a bay leaf and a little salt. When the vegetables are tender, simmer the sauce without a cover on the pan for 20 minutes. Strain the sauce, discarding the vegetables. It will keep for a few days in the refrigerator or for several months if frozen. Vegetarian broth granules, available in health food stores, are convenient and can make excellent stock.

TVP® Recipes

Breakfast

"Sausage" Gravy on Biscuits

A great breakfast dish that can be made the night before and reheated in a microwave.

Yields about 1 quart, enough for 16 biscuits.

Stir together and set aside:
- **1 cup TVP® granules**
- **7/8 cup hot water**
- **1 Tbsp. tamari**

Toast in a heavy-bottomed pan for 10-15 minutes, until you can smell the aroma, stirring occasionally so as not to scorch:
- **1/2 cup flour**

Stir into the flour and continue cooking a few minutes:
- **1/4 cup bland vegetable oil or margarine**

Slowly stir in, whisking to avoid lumps:
- **4 cups warm vegetable stock**
- **2 tsp. powdered sage**
- **1 tsp. marjoram**
- **1/2 tsp. salt**
- **1/4 tsp. black pepper**

Simmer gravy, when it bubbles stir in the **TVP®**. To serve, split a hot biscuit and top with about **1/4 cup of the gravy.**

Per 1/4 Cup Serving: Calories: 59, Protein: 3 gm., Carbohydrates: 4 gm., Fat: 4 gm

TVP® Recipes

TVP Recipes

Appetizers

TVP® Recipes

TVP® Recipes

TVP® Recipes

Dolmas (Stuffed Grape Leaves)

Makes about 36

Rinse and drain:
   1 (1 lb.) jar grape leaves

Sauté until tender:
   1 cup onion, finely chopped
   1 clove garlic, minced
   2 Tbsp. olive oil

Combine for filling:
   1 cup TVP® granules or flakes mixed with 7/8 cup hot water
   1 cup cooked brown rice
   the cooked onion
   2 Tbsp. fresh mint, chopped
   1/4 cup fresh parsley, minced
   1 tsp. salt
   1/2 tsp. cinnamon
   1/4 tsp. black pepper
   1 tsp. honey
   2 Tbsp. lemon juice

Place about 2 teaspoons stuffing in the center of each leaf, on the vein side. Fold up bottom of leaf, fold sides in and roll toward tip into a firm roll. Brush the bottom of a deep heavy-bottomed pan with oil, add slices of lemon, then place a layer of rolls folded side down. Place the next layer of rolls carefully on top. Place a pan or dinner plate on top of the rolls and weight it down with some heavy canned goods. This prevents rolls opening up. Add 2 cups hot vegetable stock. Cover, bring to a boil, then reduce heat and simmer 30 minutes. Cool before removing from pan. Serve warm or cold.

Per Dolma: Calories: 21, Protein: 1 gm., Carbohydrates: 2 gm., Fat: 1 gm.

Chinese Barbecued Chunks

*Spicy and aromatic. Serve with toothpicks as an appetizer
or mix with cooked rice for a main dish.*

Makes about 1 quart - serves 8

Combine in a 2-quart pan or bowl:
**2 cups TVP® chunks
2 cups boiling water
2 Tbsp. ketchup**

Let stand for 10 minutes. Cover tightly and microwave on medium for 10 minutes or simmer top of stove 20 minutes, adding
more liquid if needed.

Mix in a small pan:
**1/3 cup ketchup
1/4 cup brown sugar
2 Tbsp. dark sesame oil
2 Tbsp. tamari
2 tsp. 5 spice powder***

Heat sauce, adding any liquid from the chunks. Stir well and
when sauce is boiling, mix with the chunks. Let marinate 30
minutes or more. Before serving, bake in the marinade in a covered dish in a microwave on medium power about 5 minutes,
stirring once. Or bake at 350° about 15 minutes until chunks and
sauce are hot. Serve with toothpicks.

*5 spice powder contains Schezchwan pepper so is "hot". It can be obtained at health
food stores or oriental markets, or you can make your own version, (See Ingredients,
page 7)

Per Appetizer Serving: Calories: 53, Protein: 4 gm., Carbohydrates: 7 gm., Fat: 2 gm.

Party Paté

A fancy French paté might feature strips of elegant and very expensive truffles; we've achieved the look and texture of truffles by studding our paté with small strips of shiitake mushrooms. To achieve firmness for slicing, the paté must be weighted down as it cools.

Makes 1 3/4 lbs.

Soak overnight in 3 cups of water:
1 cup dried pinto beans, rinsed

Rinse, drain, add 3 cups fresh water and:
1 bay leaf
5 cloves garlic, smashed and peeled

Bring to a boil and cook 70-80 minutes until tender. Remove bay leaf and drain.

Mix 7/8 cup hot water with:
1 cup TVP® granules or flakes
1 Tbsp. ketchup

Set **TVP®** aside and stir into the beans:
1 tsp. salt
1 tsp. marjoram
1 tsp. oregano

Sauté or cook in a microwave until soft:
1 Tbsp. olive oil
1/2 cup chopped onion

Pour 1 cup hot water over:
3 large dried shiitake mushrooms

When mushrooms have soaked for 15 minutes, remove and slice into 1" strips about 1/4" wide. Set mushrooms aside to fold in last.

Combine in a food processor or blender:
the drained, cooked beans
the cooked onion
the rehydrated TVP®
2 Tbsp. mirin
1 Tbsp. tamari
1/4 tsp. ground black pepper
1 tsp. mace

Blend until the mixture is smooth, adding a little water if mixture appears dry. Taste and adjust seasonings. Fold in (but do not process) the mushroom strips. Pack mixture into a lightly oiled 1 quart mold. Some mushroom strips can be arranged on the bottom of the mold.

To cook in a microwave, cover tightly with plastic wrap, pierce wrap in one place with the tip of a sharp knife and microwave on full power for 10 minutes.

To cook in a coventional oven, cover paté with foil and place mold in a pan of hot water. Bake at 350° for 1 hour.

Remove from oven or microwave, place a plate or foil covered cardboard cut to fit on top of paté and weight down until paté becomes firm. Let paté cool in refrigerator. Run a sharp knife around sides to loosen and unmold.

To serve 8 as an appetizer, slice evenly and place each slice on leaves of Boston lettuce, garnish plate with a curl of split green onion or cornichons. Paté would serve 28 if used as a spread on thin slices of melba toast or on crackers.

Per 1 oz. Serving: Calories: 38, Protein: 3 gm., Carbohydrates: 6 gm., Fat: 1 gm.

Stuffed Mushrooms

Serves as an easy first course or entree.

18 appetizers or serves 6 as a main course.

Place in a bowl and let stand 5 minutes:
**1 cup TVP® granules or flakes
7/8 cup boiling water**

Rinse, wipe dry, and remove stems from
18 large mushrooms (about 1 1/4 pounds)

Chop the stems. Heat a skillet, add:
2 Tbsp. margarine or oil

Sauté the stems over medium high heat a few minutes, adding:
2 garlic cloves, finely chopped

Add the mushrooms and garlic to the **TVP®** with:
**1 cup fine bread crumbs
1/2 cup walnuts, chopped (optional)
1/4 cup parsley, finely chopped
1 tsp. salt
1 tsp. sage
1/2 tsp. marjoram
1/4 tsp. black pepper**

Place mushroom caps in a lightly oiled baking dish. Spoon stuffing into caps, mounding on top. Bake at 350° about 25 minutes, or cover tightly with plastic wrap and microwave on high for 10 to 12 minutes.

Per Appetizer Serving: Calories: 53, Protein: 4 gm., Carbohydrates: 7 gm., Fat: 2 gm.

TVP® Recipes

TVP® Recipes

Soups

TVP® Recipes

TVP® Recipes

TVP® Recipes

Noodle Soup

A nourishing easy-to-make soup that children like.

Serves 6

Heat a large pan and sauté:
   1 cup onion (1 medium), chopped
   2 Tbsp. olive oil

When onion is soft and beginning to brown, add:
   6 cups hot water
   1 cup TVP® granules or flakes
   2 cups noodles (broken)
   1 tsp. salt

Bring the soup to a brisk boil and cook 10-15 minutes. Stir in:
   1/4 cup nutritional yeast flakes (See ingredients, page 7)

Ladle into bowls and top with chopped parsley if desired.

Per Serving: Calories: 172, Protein: 10 gm., Carbohydrates: 21 gm., Fat: 6 gm.

Chuckwagon Soup

Robust in flavor, simple to make.

Serves 6

Stir together and set aside:
1 cup TVP® granules or flakes
3/4 cup hot water
1 Tbsp. ketchup

Heat a large kettle and cook for 5 to 10 minutes:
2 Tbsp. olive oil
1 large onion, chopped

Add the **TVP®** to the kettle with:
2 cloves garlic, smashed and chopped
1 (16 oz.) can tomatoes, diced
4 cups hot vegetable stock or broth
1 tsp. basil
1 tsp. oregano
1 tsp. salt

When soup begins to boil, drop in:
1 (10 oz.) package mixed frozen vegetables

Simmer soup until vegetables are tender, about another 10 minutes. You may wish to sprinkle with **nutritional yeast flakes** (See Ingredients, page 7).

Per Serving: Calories: 180, Protein: 13 gms., Carbohydrates: 24 gm., Fat: 6 gm.

Lentil Soup

A satisfying soup, high in protein and flavor, low in calories.

Makes 7 cups

Cook in a large pan 15-20 minutes:
- **1 cup dried lentils**
- **6 cups water**
- **1 large carrot, diced**
- **1 bay leaf**

Sauté until softened:
- **2 Tbsp. olive oil**
- **1 medium onion, chopped**
- **2 cloves garlic, mashed, chopped**
- **1 cup celery, chopped**

Add vegetables to the cooking lentils, with:
- **1 cup TVP® granules or flakes**
- **2 Tbsp. tamari**
- **2 Tbsp. tomato paste**

Cook 20-30 minutes more, until lentils are soft. Taste and adjust seasonings, adding a little salt or a pinch of cayenne if desired.

Per 1 Cup Serving: Calories: 157, Protein: 11 gm., Carbohydrates: 21 gm., Fat: 4 gm.

Minestrone

A hearty meal-in-a-bowl soup.

Serves 8

Soak overnight in a quart of water, then drain and rinse:
- **1 cup dried pinto or red kidney beans**

Simmer for 1 hour or until tender:
the soaked beans
3 cloves garlic, crushed
1 bay leaf
1 quart water

After 45 minutes, add to the beans and continue cooking until beans are tender, adding more liquid if needed:
1 cup TVP® granules or flakes

Sauté in another kettle until soft:
1 cup onion (1 medium), chopped
2 Tbsp. olive oil

Add to kettle:
3 carrots, scrubbed, diced
1 quart hot vegetable stock

Bring to a boil, reduce heat to a simmer, cover pan and cook 15 minutes. Add:
1 (16 oz.) can tomatoes, cut up
1 cup fresh or frozen peas or diced zucchini
1 tsp. salt
1 tsp. oregano
1 tsp. basil
1/2 tsp. marjoram
1 cup leftover cooked pasta or rice
the hot cooked beans with liquid and TVP®

Simmer 15 minutes, taste, and add salt and pepper if desired. Serve in big bowls. Sprinkle on top either **nutritional yeast flakes** (See ingredients, page 7) **or grated soy parmesan cheese** .

Per Serving: Calories: 191, Protein: 12 gm., Carbohydrates: 29 gm., Fat: 3 gm.

Country Chili

Flakes work nicely in this. If you don't have any on hand, you can make them by whizzing the larger chunks in a blender for a second or two. Or use larger chunks, soaking before adding. Freeze leftover chili.

Makes about 4 quarts (serves 10)

Pour 2 cups boiling water over and let stand 10 minutes:
- **2 cups TVP® flakes or chunks**
- **2 Tbsp. ketchup**

Prepare:
- **1 large onion, chopped**
- **1 green pepper, chopped**
- **2 cloves garlic, chopped**
- **1 jalapeño pepper, chopped (optional)**

Heat a large Dutch oven. Add:
- **2 Tbsp. olive oil**

Over medium heat, sauté the onions, pepper and garlic a few minutes. Sprinkle over the **TVP®** and stir with a fork:
- **2 Tbsp. chili powder**
- **2 tsp. cumin**
- **2 tsp. oregano**
- **1/2 tsp. cayenne**

Add the **TVP®** to the pan and cook a few minutes. Stir in:
- **2 (28 oz.) cans tomatoes, coarsely chopped**
- **2 (16 oz.) cans red kidney beans with liquid**
- **2 cups hot water or vegetable broth**

Cover and simmer for 30 minutes to one hour. Taste and add salt. If desired, add a **16 oz. package of frozen corn** for the last 15 minutes.

Per Serving: Calories: 198, Protein: 14 gm., Carbohydrates: 31 gm., Fat: 3 gm.

TVP® Recipes

TVP® Recipes

Sandwiches

TVP® Recipes

TVP® Recipes

TVP® Recipes

Chili Dog Rolls

These can be eaten out of hand and are great for lunchboxes or picnics.

Makes 20 rolls

Dissolve in a large bowl and let stand a few minutes:
- **1 Tbsp. dry yeast**
- **1/4 cup warm water**
- **1/2 tsp. sugar or honey**

Add:
- **1 cup warm water**
- **1 Tbsp. olive oil**

Stir in:
- **4 cups unbleached or whole wheat flour**

Turn dough out onto a work surface and knead for 5 minutes or more until smooth, adding more flour if needed. Cover and let rise for an hour.

For the filling, mix:
- **7/8 cup boiling water**
- **1 cup TVP® granules or flakes**

Let stand while preparing vegetables:
- **1 medium onion, chopped**
- **1/2 green pepper, chopped**
- **1 clove garlic, minced**
- **1 cup mushrooms (6 large), chopped, (optional)**

Heat a non-stick skillet, add:
- **2 tsp. olive oil**

Sauté the onions, pepper, and garlic a few minutes to soften, then remove to a bowl.

Heat the pan, add:
- **1 Tbsp. olive oil**

Sauté the reconstituted **TVP**® a minute or two, sprinkling with:

1 tsp. cumin
2 tsp. chili powder
1 tsp. oregano
1/2 tsp. salt

Cook a few minutes with the spices. Add:

1 large tomato, chopped
**   or 1 (8 oz.) can tomato sauce**

Combine the onions, peppers, mushrooms, **TVP**®, and tomato. Punch down the risen dough and divide into 2 balls. Have 2 lightly oiled baking sheets ready. On a lightly floured surface, roll a ball of dough out into a long oblong, about 5 inches wide. Spread half the filling down the long side of the dough, leaving edges bare. Roll dough over to seal filling in, pinching edges. Cut each roll of dough into 10 pieces, placing slices on baking sheets, seam side down. Let rise again for 20 minutes. Heat oven to 375° and bake for 20-25 minutes until lightly browned. Cool on a rack.

Per Roll: Calories: 111, Protein: 4 gm., Carbohydrates: 19 gm., Fat: 2 gm.

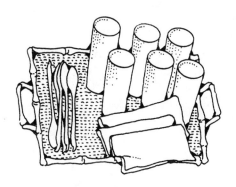

Veggie Burgers

This recipe can easily be doubled to make a dozen burgers.

Makes 6 burgers

Combine in a medium sized bowl:
- **1 cup TVP® granules**
- **3/4 cup hot water**
- **1 Tbsp. ketchup**
- **1 tsp. salt**
- **1/2 tsp. each oregano, marjoram, and garlic powder**

Let stand 10 minutes, then mix with:
- **1/4 cup carrot, grated**
- **1/4 cup celery, finely chopped**
- **2 Tbsp. green onion, finely chopped**
- **2 Tbsp. parsley, finely chopped**

Stir in to make a firm mixture:
- **1/2 cup instant gluten flour** (See ingredients, page 7)
  - **or 1/4 cup unbleached or whole wheat flour**

Instant gluten flour will give you a chewier burger but regular wheat flour will work fine.

Press mixture firmly into 6 flat patties, about 4" wide, using about 1/2 cup of the mixture for each patty. Heat a skillet and add:
- **2 Tbsp. oil**

Fry patties for 8-10 minutes on a side over medium low heat until browned. Serve in buns.

Per Burger: Calories: 129, Protein: 12 gm., Carbohydrates: 11 gm., Fat: 5 gm.

Sloppy Joes

Serves 8

Have ready:
- **8 large Kaiser or hard rolls, split**
- **2 cups TVP® granules or flakes mixed with 1 3/4 cups hot water**
- **1 Tbsp. olive oil**
- **2 cloves garlic, minced**
- **1 onion, chopped**
- **1 green pepper, chopped**
- **6 oz. can tomato paste**
- **1/2 cup water**
- **1 tsp. oregano**
- **1/4 cup ketchup**
- **1/4 tsp. cayenne**
- **1 tsp. Worcestershire sauce**
- **1 Tbsp. honey (optional)**
- **Shredded lettuce**

Heat a skillet, add the oil, and when it is hot sauté quickly the garlic, onions, peppers, and **TVP®**. Mix the tomato paste with the water and seasonings and stir into the pan. Bring to a boil, taste and add salt if desired. Sauce should be thick but spreadable; add a little more water if needed. Split the buns in half, toasting if desired. Spoon sauce on bottom half of bun, pile on lettuce and top with remaining bun half.

Per Serving: Calories: 266, Protein: 17 gm., Carbohydrates: 45 gm., Fat: 2 gm.

Gyros

A marvelous Greek sandwich served in pita pockets
Serves 6

Soak for 10 minutes:
1 cup TVP® chunks or slices
1 Tbsp. ketchup
1 cup boiling water

Cover tightly and microwave on high for 5 minutes or add 1/2 cup water or vegetable stock and simmer on top of stove 15-20 minutes until tender. Chill.

Mix for a dressing:
1/4 cup olive oil
1 Tbsp. wine vinegar
1 tsp. each salt, basil, and oregano
1/4 tsp. white or black pepper

Mix marinade with cooked drained **TVP®**. (If desired, double the amount of dressing and marinate the drained **TVP®** overnight).

Prepare the vegetables:
1 large tomato, diced
1 cucumber, thinly sliced
1/2 cup red onion, chopped
1/4 cup Greek Kalamata olives, sliced
2 Tbsp. fresh mint leaves, chopped
3 cups lettuce, shredded

Have ready, warmed in oven if desired:
6 pita breads, cut in half

Toss the vegetables with the **TVP®**. Fill pita pockets.

Per Serving: Calories: 290, Protein: 12 gm., Carbohydrates: 32 gm., Fat: 9 gm.

Devilled Burgers

Topping can be prepared in advance as it keeps well in refrigerator. Accompany these with soup or salad for a filling meal.

Serves 8

Have ready:
8 whole wheat buns, split in half

Mix and let stand 10 minutes:
2 cups TVP® granules or flakes
1 3/4 cup boiling water

Mix in another bowl for a sauce:
6 oz. can tomato paste
1/2 cup vegetable stock or water
1/2 tsp. salt
1 tsp. oregano
1 tsp. cumin
1 tsp. Worcestershire sauce
1/2 tsp. red hot sauce

Stir the **TVP®** into the sauce, adding a little more liquid if needed to make it spreadable. Place buns on a cookie sheet, spread with **TVP®** mixture and run under a preheated broiler, cooking 4 to 5 minutes until topping is bubbly. Be sure to spread mixture all the way to the edges so the buns don't burn.

Per Burger: Calories: 166, Protein: 14 gm., Carbohydrates: 27 gm., Fat: 1 gm.

French Bread Vegetable Pizzas

Serves 4

Preheat oven to 375°.

Slit in half lengthwise, then cut in half and place on a baking sheet:
1 long loaf French bread

Soak in a bowl for 5 minutes:
1 cup TVP® granules
7/8 cup boiling water

Slice thinly into a pyrex bowl or quart measure:
1 large onion
1 green pepper
1 small zucchini

Cover the vegetables with plastic wrap and place in microwave on high for 2 minutes. Remove. Or soften vegetables by placing in a steamer basket over boiling water for 2 minutes.

Add to the vegetables:
1 cup sliced mushrooms

Heat a skillet and add:
2 Tbsp. olive oil

Sauté the reconstituted **TVP®**, stirring lightly. Mix it with:
1 (14 oz.) jar pizza sauce

Spread **TVP®** sauce on the bread. Divide the vegetables onto the 4 pieces.

Mix herbs:
1 Tbsp. each oregano and basil
1 tsp. fennel seeds (optional)
1/4 tsp. red pepper flakes

Sprinkle herbs on top of vegetables. If desired, top with:
  4 oz. shredded soy mozzarella cheese.

Bake at 375° for 15-20 minutes.

Per Serving: Calories: 317, Protein: 18 gm., Carbohydrates: 47 gm., Fat: 8 gm.

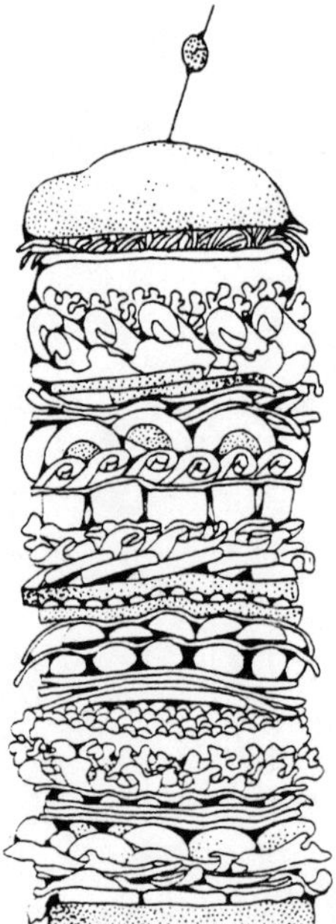

Main Dishes

Hearty Baked Beans

These are easy to make in a microwave, or you can oven-bake them in a beanpot country style.

Serves 8

Stir together and let stand 10 minutes:

2 cups TVP® granules or flakes
1 3/4 cup hot water
2 Tbsp. ketchup

Place in a 3-quart casserole, cover with plastic wrap and micro-wave for 2 minutes on high, or sauté a few minutes on top of stove:

1 Tbsp. peanut oil
1 medium onion (about 1 cup), chopped

Stir into the onions:

2 (16 oz.) cans vegetarian beans in tomato sauce
1 to 2 Tbsp. molasses or sorghum

Stir the **TVP®** into the beans. Cover casserole with plastic wrap and pierce it in 3 places. Microwave on high for 3 minutes, remove cover and stir. Microwave on high 3 minutes more.

Or cover casserole with foil and bake at 350° about 30 minutes.

Per Serving: Calories: 210, Protein: 19 gm., Carbohydrates: 32 gm., Fat: 2 gm.

Baked Stuffed Vidalia Onions

A delectable way to take advantage of this seasonal vegetable.

Serves 4

Peel, slice off the top and hollow out, leaving about a 1/2" thick shell:

4 flat Vidalia onions (about 1 1/2 pounds total)

Place shells in a baking dish, cover with plastic wrap and microwave on high for 5 minutes. Or place shells in a steamer basket and steam for 6 minutes after water boils. Measure 1/2 cup of the onion that has been scooped out and chop it finely. Heat a small skillet and cook the chopped onion on top of stove or in microwave until soft with: **1 tsp. olive oil**

Stir together:

1/2 cup TVP® granules or flakes
1/2 cup hot water
1/2 tsp. each marjoram, cumin and salt
pinch of cayenne

Mix the **TVP®** with the onions and stir in: **1/2 cup fine bread crumbs**

Spoon the filling into the onion shells, heaping it in mounds. Place the remaining onion scraps, coarsely cut, around the stuffed onions.

Pour into the pan:

1/2 cup vegetable stock
1/2 cup varietal grape juice or white wine

Cover tightly and microwave on high for 6 minutes. Remove dish and let stand 5 minutes. Onions are done if tender when pierced with a knife. The dish can be baked uncovered in a conventional oven at 375° for 30 to 35 minutes.

Per Serving: Calories: 183, Protein: 11 gm., Carbohydrates: 33 gm., Fat: 3 gm.

Almond Rice Casserole

A hearty dish that makes a complete meal.

Serves 6

Have ready according to the directions on page 91:

3 to 3 1/2 cups cooked brown rice (1 cup raw rice)

Combine and set aside:

1 cup TVP® granules or flakes
7/8 cup hot water
1 Tbsp. ketchup

Sauté in a skillet or in a microwave for 2 minutes:

1 Tbsp. peanut oil
1 medium onion, chopped

Mix rice, **TVP®**, cooked onions, in a 2 quart casserole with:

1/2 cup roasted almonds, sliced

Mix together and stir in:

2 Tbsp. light miso
1/2 tsp. thyme
1 tsp. marjoram
1/2 tsp. salt

For oven baking, cover casserole with foil and bake at 350° for 30 minutes. **To microwave,** cover tightly with plastic wrap and heat on high for 10 minutes.

For a mushroom variation: instead of the almonds, add **1 cup sliced fresh shiitake mushrooms** to the rice and other ingredients and bake as above.

Per Serving: Calories: 246, Protein: 12 gm., Carbohydrates: 32 gm., Fat: 9 gm.

Noodle and Corn Casserole

Kids will ask for seconds of this easy supper dish.

Serves 6

Cook according to package directions:
8 oz. medium noodles

Combine and let stand:
1 cup TVP® granules or flakes
7/8 cup hot water

Place in the bottom of a 3 quart casserole:
1 Tbsp. olive oil
1/2 cup onion, chopped

Sauté or microwave on high a few minutes to soften. Add the reconstituted **TVP®** to the dish and stir in:
1 Tbsp. tamari

Cook **TVP®** and onion 1 minute, then combine with:
1 (16 oz.) package frozen corn, drained
the drained noodles
1 cup vegetable broth

Cover tightly with plastic wrap and microwave on high 5 to 10 minutes. Pierce cover and remove. Or cover and bake at 350° about 30 minutes.

Per Serving: Calories: 288, Protein: 15 gm., Carbohydrates: 49 gm., Fat: 5 gm.

Spinach Mushroom Pie

A 16 oz. package of frozen bread dough can be used as a timesaver.

Serves 8

Make a bread dough by combining:
 1 Tbsp. dry yeast
 1 cup warm water
 1/2 tsp. sugar

Let stand 5 minutes, add:
 1 Tbsp. oil
 3 cups unbleached flour
 1/2 tsp. salt

Mix, adding flour as needed, and knead about 5 minutes into a smooth, elastic ball of dough. Cover and let rise until double. Punch down, reserve a third of the dough for the topping. If using prepared dough, let it thaw. Roll two-thirds of the dough out into a 12" circle and fit it into a 10" springform pan, patting it up the sides.

Mix for the filling:
 1 cup TVP® granules or flakes mixed with:
 7/8 cup boiling water
 1 tsp. oregano
 1 tsp. basil
 1/2 tsp. fennel seeds

Heat a skillet and add:
 1 Tbsp. olive oil

Sauté the **TVP®** and seasonings for a few minutes. Add:
 2 cups mushrooms (about 4 oz. fresh), sliced

Mix with:
 1 (10 oz.) package chopped spinach, thawed, drained
 1 (6 oz.) can tomato paste
 1/4 cup water

Spread filling onto the dough. Roll remaining dough into an 10" circle, cut it into 8 wedges. Arrange wedges on top of the filling, overlapping slightly, sealing wide ends to the bottom crust. Brush the top crust with a little bit of milk or oil. Preheat oven to 375° and bake for 30-35 minutes. If it begins to brown too much, cover with foil the last 5 or 10 minutes. Cut into 8 wedges to serve.

Note: If you don't have a springform pan, roll the dough into a large oblong, spread evenly with the filling and roll up like a jelly roll. Bake as directed above, cut into 16 slices to serve

Per Serving: Calories: 244, Protein: 12 gm., Carbohydrates: 41 gm., Fat: 4 gm.

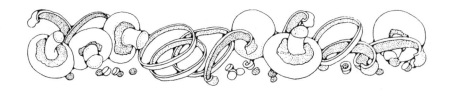

Chunks in a Creole Sauce

Serves 6-8

Combine, let stand 10 minutes, then cover tightly and microwave on medium high 10 minutes or simmer on top of stove 20 minutes until tender, adding more liquid as needed:

1 cup TVP® chunks
1 Tbsp. ketchup
1 cup boiling water

Sauté or cook in microwave 3 minutes on medium high heat:

1 Tbsp. olive oil
1 medium onion, chopped
1 green pepper, diced

Skin by dipping into boiling water, then chop:

2 fresh tomatoes
(or use 2 cups canned stewed tomatoes)

Add tomatoes to onions, plus:

1 crushed garlic, minced
1 bay leaf
1 tsp. salt
pinch of cayenne

Cover and simmer sauce over low heat 20 minutes on top of stove, 10 minutes on medium in a microwave. Add cooked chunks to sauce, cook few minutes more. Remove bay leaf. Taste and add a little more cayenne if you like it hot. Serve over rice.

Per Serving: Calories: 63, Protein: 5 gm., Carbohydrates: 8 gm., Fat: 2 gm.

Herbed Loaf

Leftover loaf can be sliced for sandwiches or a cold cut platter.

Serves 8 (16-18 slices)

Mix in a large bowl:

3 cups TVP® granules
2 1/2 cups boiling water
1/4 cup ketchup
1 tsp. basil

Let stand for 10 minutes. Microwave for 2 minutes on high or sauté until soft:

1/2 cup onion, finely chopped
2 Tbsp. olive oil

Add onions to the rehydrated **TVP®** and stir in:

1 cup instant gluten flour* (See Ingredients, page 7)
   or 3/4 cup unbleached or whole wheat flour
1 tsp. salt
1/4 tsp. pepper
1/2 tsp. each garlic powder, oregano, and marjoram
1/2 cup parsley, finely minced

Lightly oil a loaf or bread pan and pack mixture in tightly, smoothing top. Bake at 350° about 45 minutes. If loaf begins to get too brown on top, cover with foil. After removing from oven, let stand in pan 10 minutes, then run a knife round edges to loosen and turn loaf out onto a platter. Garnish with lemon slices and sprigs of parsley. Loaf can be served with **Tomato Sauce** or **Mushroom Gravy** on next 2 pages.

*Instant gluten flour has a high gluten content and makes a firm solid loaf. (See Ingredients, page 7)

Per Serving: Calories: 196, Protein: 24 gm., Carbohydrates: 21 gm., Fat: 4 gm.

Tomato Sauce

Makes about 3 cups

Heat a heavy bottomed sauce pan and sauté:

1 Tbsp. olive oil
1 medium onion, chopped (about 1 cup)
2 cloves garlic, smashed and chopped

When onions are soft and beginning to brown, add:

2 cups canned plum tomatoes, chopped
3/4 cup water or vegetable broth
1 bay leaf
1/2 tsp. salt
1/4 tsp. black pepper

Simmer over low heat, uncovered, stirring occasionally, for about 20 minutes. Add a little more water if needed. Don't let it scorch.

Remove the bay leaf and add:

1/2 tsp. oregano
1/2 tsp. basil

Cook 5 minutes more. Sauce should be thick. You can process it in a blender or food processor to make it smoother.

Per 1/4 Cup: Calories: 36, Protein: 1 gm., Carbohydrates: 6 gm., Fat: 1 gm.

Mushroom Sauce

Makes about 2 cups

Heat a heavy bottomed sauce pan and sauté together:
2 Tbsp. margarine
1 Tbsp. minced onion or shallot
4 oz. mushrooms, thinly sliced

Cook about 5 minutes, stirring occasionally. Sprinkle with:
1/4 cup flour

Stir well, then add slowly while stirring:
2 cups vegetable broth

Cook until sauce begins to bubble

Per 1/4 Cup: Calories: 54, Protein: 1 gm., Carbohydrates: 5 gm., Fat: 4 gm.

Red Beans and Rice

A no-fat cajun treat, vegetarian style

Serves 8

Soak overnight in 6 cups of water:
   2 cups dried red beans, kidney or pinto beans

Drain and rinse well.

Cook in kettle with:
   1 large onion, chopped
   6 large cloves garlic, smashed
   2 quarts boiling water

After beans have cooked 45 minutes, add:
   2 cups TVP® granules or flakes
   3 Tbsp. chili powder
   1 Tbsp. cumin

Continue cooking beans until tender, 20 to 40 minutes. Most of the liquid should have cooked into the beans and **TVP®**. Taste and add salt.

Meanwhile, cook brown rice according to the direction on page 91:
   1 cup brown rice (basmati or short grain)
   2 cups water
   1 tsp. salt

Mix the cooked rice and beans, taste, add a pinch of cayenne or hot sauce if desired.

Per Serving: Calories: 253, Protein: 20 gm., Carbohydrates: 45 gm., Fat: 0 gm.

Homestyle Hash

You may want to use two skillets for quicker cooking and more of the crispy brown crust.

Serves 6 to 8

Mix and let stand for 10 minutes:
- **1 cup TVP® granules or flakes**
- **1 Tbsp. ketchup**
- **7/8 cup boiling water**

Have ready:
- **1 (20 oz.) package shredded potatoes**
  or 4 large potatoes, peeled and grated coarsely into long, thin strands

Heat a large skillet and add:
- **1 Tbsp. oil**

Over medium high heat, sauté the reconstituted **TVP®** with:
- **1/2 cup onion, chopped**

Mix **TVP®** with potatoes. Add a little more oil (1-2 Tbsp.) to the hot skillet. Pat mixture into an even layer, reduce heat and cook 10-15 minutes. Turn over carefully and cook the other side. Sometimes it is easier to cut the cooking hash into 4 wedges to turn.

Sprinkle with:
- **2 Tbsp. parsley, finely chopped**

Cut into wedges to serve.

Per Serving: Calories: 123, Protein: 8 gm., Carbohydrates: 20 gm., Fat: 2 gm.

Stuffed Cabbage Rolls

An ethnic dish with a robust flavor.

Makes 12 rolls

Remove center core from a large head of cabbage. Place head in a colander and pour hot water over to loosen leaves, or microwave the whole head for 5 minutes on high. Cool slightly and remove 12 leaves. Remove hard center rib from each leaf.

Soak for 15 minutes:

4 large dried shiitake mushrooms
1 cup boiling water

Remove mushrooms and chop, discarding stems.

Combine:

1 cup TVP® granules
7/8 cup boiling water
1 Tbsp. ketchup

Heat a pan and sauté until soft or microwave 2 minutes:

1 cup onion (1 medium), chopped
1 clove garlic, minced
1 Tbsp. olive oil

Combine for the filling:

1 cup cooked brown rice (See Instructions, page 91)
the chopped shiitake mushrooms
the softened onion and garlic
the soaked TVP®
1 tsp. salt
1/4 tsp. mace or nutmeg
1/2 tsp. coriander

Place each cabbage leaf on a work surface, outside down. Fill with about 2 tablespoons of **TVP®** mixture, fold sides of leaf into center and roll up. Place seam side down in a lightly oiled 11" x 9" x 3" dish.

For the sauce, whiz in a blender:

1 (16 oz.) can tomatoes
1 tsp. honey

Spoon sauce over rolls. **For oven baking,** cover with foil and bake at 350° for 35-40 minutes. **For microwave,** cover tightly with plastic wrap and cook on medium high for 15 minutes; pierce plastic to release steam and uncover.

Per Roll: Calories: 74, Protein: 5 gm., Carbohydrates: 12 gm., Fat: 1 gm.

Variations

Stuffed Green Peppers

Cut **4 green peppers** in halves lengthwise, removing seeds and membranes. Fill pepper halves with the cabbage roll stuffing, place in an oiled dish and add **1 cup of hot water** around base of peppers. Top with the sauce. Follow the baking or microwave directions for the cabbage rolls.

Stuffed Zucchini

Trim ends of **6 zucchini**, cut in halves lengthwise. Carefully scoop out centers, leaving quarter-inch thick shells. Chop the pulp and add to the cabbage roll filling. Stuff the shells, place in a baking pan, and add **1/4 cup water** to pan. Top with the sauce. Follow baking or microwave directions for cabbage rolls.

Stuffed Eggplant

Try using Japanese, Chinese, or Middle Eastern eggplants. They come in several colors besides purple and make an attractive serving.

Serves 8

Cook in boiling water 10 minutes, drain and cool:

4 small eggplants

Cut each in half lengthwise, remove the flesh, leaving a shell about 1/4" thick. Chop the flesh, combine with:

1/2 cup chopped onion

Sauté eggplant and onion in **1 Tbsp. olive oil** until onion is soft.

Mix:

1/2 cup TVP®
3/8 cup boiling water
1/2 tsp. cumin
1/2 tsp. oregano
1/2 tsp. salt
juice of 1 lemon

Add to the eggplant mixture. Taste and add dash of pepper. Spoon mixture into shells, place in lightly oiled pan. Sprinkle on **1 cup soft bread crumbs** (2 slices of whole wheat bread crumbled in blender) and bake at 350° for 35-40 minutes. **Or microwave** on high for 10 minutes. Serve with **Tomato Sauce** (page 42).

Per Roll: Calories: 74, Protein: 5 gm., Carbohydrates: 12 gm., Fat: 1 gm.

Stroganoff

Chunks in a well flavored creamy sauce with mushrooms and onions

Serves 6

Combine and let stand 10 minutes, then simmer 20 minutes on top of stove or cover tightly and microwave on medium for 10 minutes:

1 cup TVP® chunks
2 Tbsp. ketchup
1 1/2 cups hot water

Cook over low heat about 15 minutes **or microwave** for 3 minutes:

2 Tbsp. margarine
1 cup onions, thinly sliced

Add to the onions and cook a few minutes more:

1 cup mushrooms, sliced

Make the sauce in another pan, heating:

1 Tbsp. margarine

Add and cook a minute or two:

1 Tbsp. flour

Stir in and cook until bubbly:

1 cup vegetable broth

Stir in:

1 Tbsp. ketchup
2 Tbsp. dairy-free sour cream

Taste sauce and add a little salt if desired. Add the cooked drained **TVP®**, and the onions, and mushrooms. Serve over noodles or hot rice.

Per Serving: Calories: 136, Protein: 11 gm., Carbohydrates: 12 gm., Fat: 4 gm.

Shepherd's Pie

Serves 6

Soak for 10 minutes:
- **2 cups TVP® chunks**
- **2 Tbsp. ketchup**
- **4 cups hot water**

Cover pan and simmer about 20 minutes, until tender.

Meanwhile, boil:
- **4 potatoes, cut up into medium size chunks**
- **water to cover**

Heat a skillet, add:
- **2 Tbsp. olive oil**

Sauté a few minutes:
- **1 cup onion (1 medium), chopped**

Add and cook a few minutes:
- **1/2 cup celery, chopped**

Sprinkle on top and stir in:
- **1/4 cup flour**

Stir and cook a few minutes, then slowly add:
- **2 cups liquid (potato water, carrot water or vegetable broth)**

When the sauce bubbles up, taste and add seasonings:
- **1/2 tsp. salt**
- **1/2 tsp oregano or thyme**
- **1/2 tsp. marjoram**
- **1/2 tsp. garlic powder**

Combine sauce and chunks with:
- **1 1/2 cups cooked carrots, sliced**
- **1 cup frozen or fresh peas**

Pour into a 3 quart casserole dish. Drain the potatoes, mash, and add:

1 Tbsp. olive oil or margarine
1/2 tsp. salt
enough milk to make smooth and spreadable

Spread potatoes on top of pie and sprinkle with paprika. Preheat oven to 350° and bake pie about 30 minutes. You may need to place the pie on a cookie sheet so it doesn't boil over in the oven. If pie has been made ahead and chilled, bake longer until filling is bubbly.

Per Serving: Calories: 231, Protein: 14 gm., Carbohydrates: 32 gm., Fat: 7 gm.

THYME

Sauerbraten

Marinating overnight gives a distinctive flavor.

Serves 6

Soak for 5 minutes:
   1 cup TVP® chunks
   1 Tbsp. ketchup
   1 cup hot water

Cover tightly and microwave on medium 5 to 10 minutes, adding water or vegetable stock if needed. Or add 1 cup liquid and simmer on top of stove about 20 minutes until tender.

Combine in a pyrex bowl or pan:
   1/2 cup cider vinegar
   1/2 cup water or stock
   1 Tbsp. honey
   1 bay leaf
   1/2 tsp. whole cloves

Bring mixture to a boil, then add cooked chunks. Remove from heat. Cover and let soak overnight in the refrigerator. Drain chunks.

Add to the remaining marinade:
   1 Tbsp. arrowroot or cornstarch
   2 Tbsp. tamari
   1/2 cup dairy-free sour cream or yogurt

Heat a skillet, add:
   2 Tbsp. oil

Add the drained **TVP®** chunks and cook until heated through, then stir in the sauce and cook a few minutes more. Serve on cooked noodles or brown rice.

Per Serving: Calories: 116, Protein: 6 gm., Carbohydrates: 10 gm., Fat: 7 gm.

Mushroom Strudel

Tender, flaky layers, easy to make.

Serves 6

Mix and let stand 5 minutes:
1 cup TVP® granules
7/8 cup hot water
1 Tbsp. ketchup

Have a pastry brush ready and:
1/2 pound filo dough, defrosted (6 to 8 sheets)
1/3 cup melted margarine or light sesame oil

Mix for filling:
1 cup fine bread crumbs
2 cups fresh shiitake mushrooms, sliced
1/4 cup onion, finely chopped
1 tsp. thyme or marjoram
1/2 tsp. salt
The 1 cup reconstituted TVP® granules

Separate filo leaves and brush 3 or 4 leaves with melted margarine or oil, stacking one on top of the other. Sprinkle **TVP®** mixture evenly over top of stack. Top with 3-4 more filo leaves, brushing each with margarine or oil. Roll up like a jelly roll, brush top with margarine. Sprinkle top with poppy seeds if desired. Place on a lightly oiled baking sheet, seam side down. Cut through roll with a sharp knife almost to the bottom to make separating into 12 slices later easier. Preheat oven to 375° and bake strudel 25 to 30 minutes. Serve with *Mushroom Sauce* (page 43).

Per Serving: Calories: 307, Protein: 13 gm., Carbohydrates: 40 gm., Fat: 10 gm.

Lasagne

The classic Italian favorite.

Serves 8

To prepare the sauce pour over and set aside:
   1 cup granular or flake TVP®
   7/8 cup boiling water

Sauté:
   1 Tbsp. olive oil
   1/2 cup onion, chopped

When onion is soft, add:
   1 (28 oz.) can tomatoes, whizzed in blender
   2 Tbsp. minced parsley
   1 tsp. oregano
   1 tsp. marjoram

Simmer, uncovered, about 20 minutes. Add **TVP®**.

Cook until tender:
   12 lasagne noodles

Drain noodles and rinse several times with cold water. Arrange a single layer of noodles on the bottom of a lightly oiled 13" x 9" x 2" pan. Top with half of the sauce. Arrange 4 more noodles, then a layer of:

   15 oz. tofu, wrapped in a towel, pressed, and crumbled

Arrange remaining noodles on top and pour on the rest of the sauce. If desired, sprinkle with **1 cup shredded soy mozarella cheese** or **2 cups** *Nutritional Yeast "Cheeze" Sauce* (next page). Cover and bake at 350° for 30 minutes. Uncover, bake 10 minutes more. Let stand 5 minutes before serving.

Per Serving: Calories: 313, Protein: 18 gm., Carbohydrates: 48 gm., Fat: 7 gm.

Variation

Lasagne Florentine

Cook 1 pound of wide green noodles according to package instructions.

Thaw and drain well:
1 (10 oz.) package chopped spinach

Arrange a layer of noodles on the bottom of the lightly oiled pan, then a layer of spinach, another layer of noodles, part of the sauce, another layer of noodles, then a layer of tofu or ricotta, topped with noodles and the remaining sauce. Top with grated mozerella or *Nutritional Yeast "Cheeze" Sauce* (below). Bake as directed.

Nutritional Yeast "Cheeze" Sauce

Makes about 2 cups

Whisk together in a heavy bottomed sauce pan:
1/2 cup nutritional yeast flakes (See Ingredients, page 7)
1/2 cup unbleached flour
1 tsp. salt

Place pan over medium high heat and whisk in: **2 cups cold water**

Continue whisking as sauce thickens, bring to a rolling boil, reduce heat, cook 1 minute, remove from heat.

Whisk in:
1/4 cup margarine or oil
1 tsp. wet mustard

Sauce will thicken as it cools, but thins down when heated.

Per 1/4 Cup Serving: Calories: 110, Protein: 1 gm., Carbohydrates: 8 gm., Fat: 7 gm.

Spaghetti Sauce

*An old favorite. You may wish to omit the **TVP**® from the sauce and use it to make balls to serve with the sauce and pasta.*

Serves 6 to 8

Combine and let stand while preparing the marinara sauce:
- **1 3/4 cup boiling water**
- **2 cups granular or flake TVP®**

Sauce can be made in a 2-quart casserole dish in the microwave, or heat a skillet to sauté:
- **1 Tbsp. olive oil**
- **1 cup onions (1 medium), chopped small**
- **2 cloves garlic, crushed**

When onions are soft, add:
- **1 (28 oz.) can plum tomatoes, chopped in blender**
- **1 tsp. oregano**
- **1 tsp. basil**
- **1 tsp. salt**
- **1/4 cup red wine (optional)**

Cover with plastic and simmer sauce for 5 minutes in a micro-wave. Or simmer on top of stove for 20 minutes. If desired, add:
- **1 cup mushrooms, chopped**

Stir in the reconstituted **TVP**® and simmer another 2 minutes in a microwave, or 5 minutes top of stove.

Cook according to package directions:
- **1 lb. spaghetti or linguine**

Drain the pasta and serve topped with sauce.

Per Serving: Calories: 297, Protein: 20 gm., Carbohydrates: 52 gm., Fat: 2 gm.

Italian Spaghetti Balls

This mixture can also be shaped into patties or burgers and served in buns.

Makes 20 balls

Mix and let stand for 10 minutes:
  2 cups TVP® granules
  1 3/4 cup boiling water

Sauté in a skillet or microwave on high for a few minutes:
  2 Tbsp. olive oil
  1/2 cup onion, chopped small

Add the **TVP®** and stir in:
  1/2 tsp. chili powder
  1/2 tsp. garlic powder
  1/2 tsp. oregano
  1 tsp. salt
  1 Tbsp. tamari

Mix in:
  1/2 cup unbleached flour
  or instant gluten flour (See Ingredients, page 7)

Mix well and shape into 1 1/2" balls, pressing firmly. When balls are made, brown lightly in a little bit of oil in a hot skillet, rolling over carefully to keep round and to brown evenly. Serve with hot pasta and sauce. A low-fat option is to bake the balls on a cookie sheet in a 350° oven until lightly browned. Makes 20 balls.

Per Ball: Calories: 47, Protein: 5 gm., Carbohydrates: 5gm., Fat: 1 gm.

Italian Ball Sandwiches

Cut open long crusty rolls and fill with balls and spaghetti sauce.

Ragout with Herbs

Old fashioned stew flavor in a dish that can be made in the microwave.

Makes about 2 quarts (4-6 servings)

Mix in a small bowl:
- **1 cup TVP® chunks**
- **1 Tbsp. ketchup**
- **1 cup boiling water**

Let stand for 10 minutes. In a 3 quart casserole, microwave on high for 30 seconds:
- **2 Tbsp. olive oil**

Add to casserole and microwave on high for 2 minutes or sauté on stove top with the oil in a skillet:
- **2 garlic cloves, smashed**
- **1 cup onion (1 medium), coarsely chopped**

Add the **TVP®**, and remaining vegetables and herbs:
- **2 ribs celery, diced**
- **3 carrots, sliced**
- **3 potatoes, cut in chunks**
- **1 bay leaf**
- **4 cups hot vegetable broth**
- **2 Tbsp. ketchup**
- **1 tsp. salt**
- **1 tsp. oregano**
- **1 tsp. marjoram**
- **1/2 tsp. thyme**

Cover tightly with plastic wrap and cook on high for 5 minutes.* Stir, set heat to medium low and cook 15 minutes more. When potatoes and carrots are tender, remove the bay leaf. Stir in:
- **1/4 cup chopped fresh parsley**

If potatoes are omitted, ragout is good served over rice or noodles.

*For stove top cooking, sauté garlic and onion in oil 5 to 10 minutes in a large pan, add **TVP®**, vegetables, herbs, and 4 cups broth, cover and simmer about 30 minutes until vegetables are tender.

Per serving: Calories: 176, Protein: 9 gm., Fat: 6 gm., Carbohydrates: 26 gm.

Variation

Ragout Vegetable Soup

Ragout can be made into a chunky vegetable soup by the addition of 1 quart of broth. Serve in soup bowls with chunks of crusty bread.

Moussaka

A vegan version of a three layered dish that is a Mediterranean classic. Traditionally, it is served lukewarm or at room temperature, so it can be made ahead to delight your guests.

Makes 9 medium or 6 large servings

For the bottom layer, peel and slice:

1 purple eggplant (about 1 pound)

Put the slices in a large bowl, sprinkling with salt (use kosher salt if you have it). Place a plate over the slices and weight it down. Let eggplant "sweat" for 30 minutes. Rinse slices, pat dry on a towel and dredge each slice in a mixture of:

1/3 cup unbleached flour
1 tsp. paprika
1/2 tsp. salt
1/8 tsp. cayenne

Heat a non-stick pan, use a little olive oil and a pastry brush to coat the pan lightly, then fry slices quickly until lightly browned. It is all right if some flour still shows. Arrange the fried slices in a 9" x 9" pan.

For the sauce layer, stir together and set aside:

1 cup TVP® flakes or granules
7/8 cup hot water

Cook until soft in a sauce pan (or in a quart measure if using the microwave):

1 Tbsp. olive oil
1 medium large onion, chopped

Puree briefly in a blender and add to the onions:

1 (16 oz.) can stewed tomatoes
2 Tbsp. minced parsley
1 tsp. oregano
1 tsp. basil

1/2 tsp. cinnamon
1/2 tsp. nutmeg
1/2 tsp. salt

Stir in:

the reconstituted TVP®

Simmer the sauce a few minutes on top of the stove or in the microwave to blend the flavors.

For the top layer, combine in a food processor or blender:

1 pound silken tofu, well drained
1/4 cup olive oil
1/4 nutritional cup yeast flakes (See Ingredients, page 7)
1/2 tsp. salt
juice of 1 lemon (2 Tbsp.)

Process or blend until smooth and creamy. Have ready:

1 cup soft bread crumbs (2 slices whole wheat bread whizzed in a blender)

To assemble, pour the tomato sauce over the eggplant slices and cover with the bread crumbs. Spread the tofu layer evenly on top, smoothing with a spatula. Preheat the oven to 375° and bake the moussaka about 50 minutes. Top will be a light golden brown. Let it stand for at least 10 minutes after you remove it from the oven.

Per Medium Serving: Calories: 204, Protein: 12 gm., Carbohydrates: 19 gm., Fat: 10 gm.

Bean and TVP® Burritos

Makes 10 burritos

Have ready:
10 large (10") tortillas or chapatis

Soak overnight in 3 cups of water:
1 cup dried pinto beans

Drain, rinse, and cook beans until tender (about 70-90 minutes) in 3 cups of water with:
1 bay leaf
3 cloves garlic, smashed

Drain beans, but reserve the liquid in case it is needed later to thin the filling mixture.

Combine:
1/2 cup TVP® granules or flakes
1/2 cup less 1 Tbsp. hot water
1 Tbsp. hot bean liquid
2 tsp. chili powder
1 tsp. cumin
1 tsp. salt
1/2 tsp. oregano

Sauté until softened over medium high heat in a good sized skillet:
1 Tbsp. olive oil
1 cup onion (1 medium), chopped

Add the seasoned **TVP®** and cook a few minutes more. Stir in the cooked beans, then transfer mixture to a food processor or blender and mash to a fairly smooth textured filling, adding a little of the bean liquid if mixture is too thick. Taste and add a little hot sauce if desired. If done in a blender, you may need to do it in two batches, then mix the batches together.

To assemble: heat a griddle or skillet until a few drops of water dance on the surface. Dry fry each tortilla on both sides until the surface of the tortilla begins to bubble and brown slightly. Keep them warm in a thick towel. When all are heated, place about 1/3 cup of filling down one side of a tortilla and roll up. You may wish to enclose or serve with side dishes of shredded lettuce, grated soy cheese, salsa sauce or sliced avocados.

Burritos may be made ahead, kept wrapped, and baked before serving. Unwrap, place on cookie sheet, brush tops lightly with oil if desired and bake at 350° about 20 minutes.

Per Burrito: Calories: 164, Protein: 9 gm., Carbohydrates: 28 gm., Fat: 2 gm.

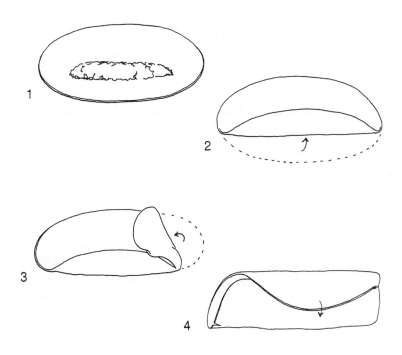

Burrito Variations:

Green Chili Burritos

Add to the filling mixture as you process or blend it:
1 (4 oz.) can chopped green chilis, mild or hot, drained

Chimichangas

Place the filling near one edge of each tortilla and fold in the sides as you roll it up so you have a neat envelope with no filling exposed. Fasten each with a toothpick. Heat at least 2 inches of oil in a deep pan or wok to 360° and fry 2 or 3 at a time until golden brown, about 2 to 3 minutes. Lift out with a slotted spoon (do not use tongs) and drain on paper towels. Remove picks and serve hot with salsa, shredded lettuce, and chopped green onions.

Tostadas

Make the filling as directed, but fry each tortilla in hot, but not smoking, oil until crisp. Drain the tortillas on paper towels. Spread each crisp tortilla with about 1/3 cup filling, then sprinkle on grated soy cheddar cheese, shredded lettuce and chopped green onions. Serve open face with side dishes of salsa sauce and guacamole if desired.

More Variations

Enchiladas

10 servings

Prepare a double recipe, making 20 large burritos with the Bean and **TVP**® filling (page 62). Place them in a large, lightly oiled baking pan that is 2 inches deep. Pour over them a recipe of **Enchilada Sauce**. Over the top, pour wide strips of **Nutritional Yeast "Cheeze" Sauce** (page 55). Bake at 350° for 20-25 minutes until sauce is bubbling.

Enchilada Sauce

Heat a large sauce pan and sauté until soft:
- **2 Tbsp. olive oil**
- **1 medium large onion (1 cup), chopped**

Sprinkle on and stir in:
- **1/4 cup flour**
- **2 Tbsp. chili powder**
- **2 tsp. cumin**
- **1 tsp. garlic powder**

Cook a few minutes, then whisk in:
- **1 quart water**
- **1 tsp. salt**

Whisk as sauce thickens and simmer for about 20 minutes, stirring occasionally.

Per 1/4 Cup: Calories: 20, Protein: 0 gm., Carbohydrates: 1 gm., Fat: 1 gm.

Picadillo with Black Beans and Rice

A tasty Mexican dish usually served on individual platters with the beans and rice garnished with fried plantains or bananas.

Serves 6 to 8

To cook the beans, soak overnight:

1 cup black beans
4 cups water

Drain, rinse beans, and add:

3 cups water
1 bay leaf

Simmer until tender, about 90 minutes.

Cook until liquid is absorbed:

2 cups brown rice
4 cups water
1 tsp. salt

Mix and set aside:

1 cup TVP® granules or flakes
7/8 cup hot water

Heat a large skillet and sauté until onion is soft:

1 cup onion (1 medium), chopped
2 cloves garlic, minced
1 green pepper, chopped
2 Tbsp. olive oil

Stir into the **TVP®**:

1 Tbsp. tamari

Add **TVP®** to the skillet and cook a few minutes with the onions. Stir in:

1 (16 oz.) can tomatoes, chopped
1 Tbsp. raisins

1 tsp. capers
1/2 tsp. salt
1/2 tsp. hot sauce

Cook and stir the mixture for a few minutes. Add the cooked beans. Taste and add a little salt or more hot sauce if needed. Arrange individual platters of brown rice topped with the black bean picadillo and garnished with fried bananas or plantains.

Per Serving: Calories: 413, Protein: 16 gm., Carbohydrates: 71 gm., Fat: 9 gm.

Fried Bananas or Plantains

Peel, cut in half, and slice lengthwise:
4 firm bananas or plantains

Heat a heavy bottomed skillet and add:
1 Tbsp. oil

When oil is sizzling hot add banana slices and cook 3 to 5 minutes. Sprinkle with lemon juice and a dash of nutmeg, turn, reduce heat and cook a few minutes more.

Tamales

Marvelous finger food that kids like. Dried corn husks and masa harina flour both are available in supermarkets. The corn husks cost very little, and will keep a long time on the pantry shelf. Soaking the husks makes them pliable for stuffing and folding. Make a big batch of tamales, they are good hot or cold.

Makes 36 to 40 tamales

Soak in cold water for 1 hour:

2 to 3 oz. dried corn husks

If some husks are left over after tamales are made, dry them out and store for another day.

For the filling, soak for 5 minutes:

1 cup TVP® granules or flakes
7/8 cup hot water

Microwave on high for 2 minutes, or sauté in a skillet:

2 Tbsp. olive oil
1/2 cup onion, chopped small
3 cloves garlic, minced
1 green pepper, chopped small

To the reconstituted **TVP®**, add:

1 Tbsp. chili powder
2 tsp. cumin
1/2 tsp. garlic salt
1/2 cup tomato puree
dash of cayenne

Mix **TVP®** and onions and heat together for 2 minutes. Taste the filling and add a little hot sauce if desired.

To make the masa dough, place in a bowl:

2 cups masa harina
1 tsp. salt

Slowly add enough warm water (about 1 1/2 cups) to make a firm but moist dough, working in as you knead the mixture:

2 Tbsp. soft margarine or oil

To form the tamales, use the palm of your hand to slap-pat the masa dough into flat patties a quarter-inch thick. Fold patty around a spoonful of filling and place in a drained corn husk. Fold the husk over to enclose the filling. If husks are small or broken, use several pieces. Place 1 cup hot water in the bottom of a kettle, place a steamer rack in the kettle and stack tamales on rack. Cover pan, bring water to a boil, reduce heat and steam tamales 45 minutes. You may want to cook them in two batches, depending on the size of your steamer.

Per Tamale: Calories: 44, Protein: 2 gm., Carbohydrates: 6 gm., Fat: 2 gm.

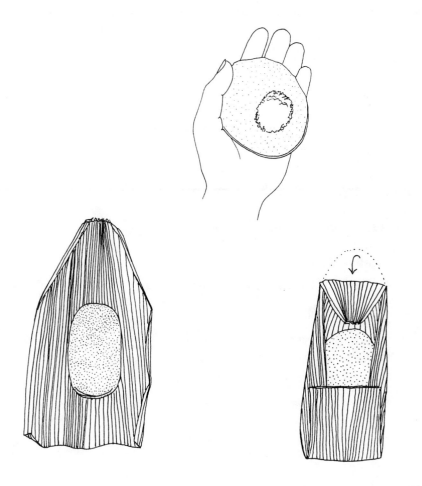

Tamale Pie

Making cornmeal mush in the microwave for the crusts of this pie is a time saver.

Serves 6 to 8

For the mush, combine in a 2 quart dish:

**1 cup yellow cornmeal
4 cups water
1 tsp. salt**

Microwave uncovered on high for 6 minutes, remove and stir, then cook 6 minutes more. Mush should be thick and bubbly. Or make mush on top of stove, preferably in the top of a double boiler, combining ingredients, and cooking 20-30 minutes after it is thickened. Whisk from time to time to prevent lumping. Lightly oil a 9" x 9" x 3" baking dish and spread half the mush for the bottom layer.

To prepare the filling, combine and set aside:

**1 cup TVP® granules or flakes
7/8 cup hot water**

Sauté until softened in skillet or microwave:

**2 Tbsp. olive oil
1 large onion, chopped
1 green pepper, chopped
1 jalapeño pepper, chopped**

Add the **TVP®** and sprinkle with:

**1 Tbsp. chili powder
2 tsp. cumin
1/2 tsp. garlic powder
1 tsp. salt**

Stir well to mix, cook a few minutes, add:

1 (16 oz.) can tomatoes, chopped

Taste to adjust seasonings, and if desired add:

1 (16 oz.) package frozen corn
a few drops hot sauce
1/4 cup black olives, sliced

Spread filling on the layer of mush and top with remaining mush, bake in a conventional oven at 350° for 30 minutes, or microwave on high for 10 minutes.

Per Serving: Calories: 221, Protein: 11 gm., Carbohydrates: 33 gm., Fat: 5 gm.

Variation

Cornbread Tamale Pie

Instead of the traditional polenta or cornmeal mush, you can make a tamale pie by spreading the filling into a 9" x 9" x 3" pan and topping it with cornbread batter.

Mix:

1 cup cornmeal
1 cup unbleached flour
2 tsp. baking powder
2 tsp. sugar
1 tsp. salt

Add:

2 Tbsp. oil
1 1/2 cups soy milk

Stir into dry ingredients. Bake at 375° about 30 minutes until cornbread begins to brown around the edges. This "pie" can be turned upside down on a platter to serve.

Empanadas

A Chilean version of turnovers, with a tasty filling wrapped in pastry.

Makes about 16-18

For the pastry, measure and mix together:
5 cups unbleached flour
2 tsp. baking powder
1 tsp. salt

Stir in with a fork, adding just enough water to shape into a ball:
3/4 cup vegetable oil
2 tsp. vinegar
1/2 to 3/4 cup ice water

Divide dough into 2 balls and chill 30 minutes before rolling out.

For the filling, combine in a bowl and let stand 10 minutes:
2 cups TVP® granules or flakes
1 3/4 cups hot water
2 Tbsp. ketchup

Sauté until soft (or microwave without the oil):
2 Tbsp. olive oil
1 cup onions, finely chopped
2 garlic, chopped

Mix the onions with the **TVP®**, stirring in:
1/3 cup pimento olives, sliced
2 Tbsp. raisins
1/2 tsp. each oregano and paprika
4 dashes hot sauce

Roll about 1/4 cup of dough into a circle 1/4" thick, 8" or 9" in diameter. Place 1/3 cup filling in the center, fold dough over and press edges together with tines of a fork. Place empanadas on an oiled baking sheet. Prick tops with fork, brush tops with soymilk. Bake at 400° 15-20 minutes until golden brown.

Per serving: Calories: 261, Protein: 9 gm., Carbohydrates: 30 gm., Fat: 12 gm.

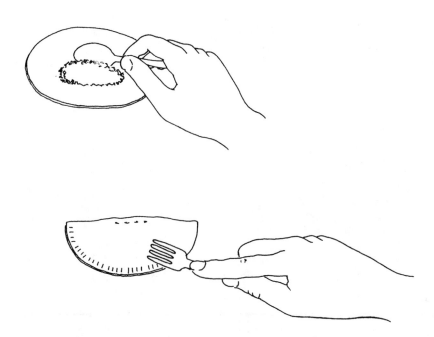

Fajitas

Let each person fill up and roll his own.

Serves 8

Combine and let stand 10 minutes:

2 cups TVP® chunks
2 1/2 cups boiling water
2 Tbsp. ketchup

Cover tightly with plastic wrap, pierce in 1 place, microwave on medium high power 10 minutes. Or increase water to 3 cups and simmer on top of stove until tender. If any excess liquid remains, drain chunks.

Cut into thin long strips:

1 large green pepper
1 large sweet red pepper

Warm by placing in a towel and a warm oven for a few minutes or in a paper towel in a microwave on high for 1 minute:

8 large whole wheat tortillas

Heat a heavy skillet and add:

1 Tbsp. olive oil

Quickly sauté the pepper strips and remove to a warm dish.

Add to hot skillet:

1 Tbsp. olive oil
the drained TVP® chunks

Stir-fry a few minutes to heat thoroughly. Place in each tortilla some **TVP®** chunks and some red and green pepper sticks, roll up, and serve. Accompany with side dishes of salsa, chopped onions, sliced avocadoes and shredded lettuce.

Per Serving: Calories: 127, Protein: 9 gm., Carbohydrates: 16 gm., Fat: 4 gm.

Spanish Rice

A one dish meal with lots of flavor. Basmati rice will add a subtle sweetness.

Serves 6

Heat a large skillet that can be tightly covered and sauté a few minutes:

> **2 Tbsp. olive oil**
> **1 medium onion, diced**
> **1 green pepper, diced**

Stir in:

> **1 cup uncooked basmati**
> **or short grain brown rice, rinsed and drained**

Cook 5 to 10 minutes, stirring frequently.

Soak:

> **1 cup granular or flake TVP®**
> **7/8 cup hot water**
> **2 cloves garlic, minced**
> **1 tsp. salt**
> **1 tsp. paprika**
> **dash of cayenne pepper**

Add to rice mixture:

> **the TVP® and spices**
> **3 cups tomato juice**

Cover pan tightly. Cook until rice is tender and has absorbed most of the liquid, stirring occasionally. Before serving, taste and add a little salt or more cayenne if needed.

Per Serving: Calories: 167, Protein: 4 gm., Carbohydrates: 27 gm., Fat: 5 gm.

Taco Salad

The filling can be made in the microwave while the shells bake in a conventional oven.

Serves 6

Heat oven to 350°. On a large cookie sheet place 6 oven-proof soup bowls.

Warm **6 large (10") tortillas** on a griddle so they are soft and flexible, or wrap in damp paper towels and microwave on high 1 minute, or set in a warm oven for 3-5 minutes. Press tortillas into the bowls, crimping edges as needed to fit. Edges can be brushed with oil if desired. Place tray in oven and bake for 12 to 15 minutes until edges begin to brown lightly. Cool shells. If not using immediately, wrap tightly in a plastic bag.

For filling, mix and let stand 5 minutes:
> **1 cup TVP® granules**
> **7/8 cup boiling water**

Sauté or heat in microwave 3 minutes:
> **1 Tbsp. olive oil**
> **1/2 cup onion, chopped**

Stir into onion:
> **1 (8 oz.) can tomato sauce**
> **1 (16 oz.) can pinto beans, drained**
> **2 tsp. chili powder**
> **1 tsp. cumin**
> **1/2 tsp. oregano**
> **the TVP®**

Mix well, cover tightly, and microwave on high for 5 minutes, stirring once. Or simmer on top of stove for 15-20 minutes.

Place a tortilla shell on each plate. Into each shell, place:
> **1/2 cup lettuce, shredded**

Spoon the hot **TVP**® sauce evenly into the shells.

Top with:
chopped fresh tomatoes
grated soy cheese (opt)
soy sour cream (opt)
sliced avocados (opt)

Per Serving: Calories: 206, Protein: 15 gm., Carbohydrates: 33 gm., Fat: 2 gm.

Mexican Molé Chunks

A classic Mexican sauce that can be mild or red hot, according to taste.

Serves 6

Soak for 5 minutes:

1 cup TVP® chunks
1 1/2 cups boiling water
1 Tbsp. ketchup

Cover tightly with plastic wrap and microwave 10 minutes on medium high power. Or simmer on top of stove 15-20 minutes until tender. Set chunks aside.

Toast in a hot dry skillet over medium high heat for about 5 minutes, flattening and stirring with a wooden spoon:

1 large dried anchos pepper, seeded and torn up

Sauté a few minutes:

1 Tbsp. safflower oil
1 medium onion, chopped
2 cloves garlic, mashed or chopped

Sprinkle onion with:

1/4 tsp. cinnamon
1/8 tsp. cloves
the pieces of anchos pepper

Stir onion and spices and add:

1 (16 oz.) can tomatoes
1/4 cup vegetable broth
1 large flour tortilla, torn up
1 oz. square unsweetened chocolate
1 tsp. honey

Cook the sauce 10 to 15 minutes, stirring occasionally. Puree in a blender until smooth, doing it in 2 batches if needed. Taste sauce and add a little salt if desired, or a dash of cayenne if you like it hotter. Return to heat, stir in the cooked **TVP**® chunks and simmer a few minutes. Serve in rolled warm tortillas or over fluffy rice. (Wrap tortillas in a paper towel and heat 1-2 minutes in a microwave or warm oven). You can also use this as a sauce to serve on baked burritos.

Per Serving: Calories: 139, Protein: 12 gm., Carbohydrates: 17 gm., Fat: 4 gm.

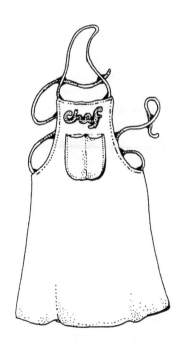

Indonesian Fried Rice

Flavors and textures blended in a Far East dish.

Serves 8

Cook until tender according to the direction on page 91:
2 cups of brown rice in 4 cups water

Turn out on a large platter to cool.

Mix and set aside:
2 cups TVP® flakes or chunks
2 cups hot water
1 Tbsp. ketchup
1 Tbsp. tamari

After the **TVP®** has soaked 5 minutes, cover tightly and microwave on medium high 6 to 10 minutes or add a little water or vegetable broth and simmer on top of stove 20-25 minutes until tender. Have ready:
1 onion, sliced in half moons
1 carrot, cut in thin match sticks
1 green pepper, cut in inch squares
1 red pepper, cut in inch squares
1 cup celery, diced
1 cup mushrooms, sliced

Heat a wok or large skillet and add:
2 Tbsp. dark sesame oil
2 cloves garlic, minced
1 Tbsp. gingerroot, minced

Add the vegetables and stir-fry over medium high heat about 5 to 8 minutes. Add the cooked **TVP®** and crumble in the cooled rice. Stir to mix and heat through, adding: **2 Tbsp. tamari**

Taste and add a little salt if needed or more soy sauce. Serve hot, topped with sliced green onions.

Per Serving: Calories: 309, Protein: 15 gm., Carbohydrates: 52 gm., Fat: 5 gm.

Bangkok Hot and Cold Salad

A crisp and colorful luncheon dish.

Serves 4 to 6

Soak for 5 minutes:
- **1 cup TVP® chunks**
- **1 Tbsp. ketchup**
- **1 cup hot water**

Cover tightly and microwave on medium high for 8-10 minutes, adding water or vegetable stock if needed, or add 1 cup liquid and simmer on top of stove 20 minutes until tender.

Combine for a marinade:
- **2 Tbsp. tamari**
- **2 Tbsp. mirin** (See Ingredients, page 7) **or sherry**
- **2 cloves garlic, crushed**
- **1 Tbsp. raw ginger, chopped**
- **1 Tbsp. cornstarch or arrowroot**

Let chunks soak in sauce while preparing vegetables.

Have ready to toss on a platter:
- **3 cups lettuce (about 1/2 head), shredded**
- **1 1/2 cups cucumber (1 medium), thinly sliced**
- **1 1/2 cups radishes (1 small bunch), sliced**

Drain the chunks and to remaining marinade add:
- **2 Tbsp. peanut butter**
- **1/2 tsp. hot red pepper sauce**
- **1/2 cup water**

Whiz sauce in blender, then bring to a boil. Stir in the chunks. When chunks are heated through, pour hot mixture over the platter of cold, crisp salad vegetables.

Per Serving: Calories: 102, Protein: 8 gm., Carbohydrates: 14 gm., Fat: 3 gm.

Indonesian Satay

These flavorful chunks can be served on toothpicks as an appetizer, threaded on skewers and broiled for the main course, or simply served on rice. This is even better made the day before.

Makes about 1 quart (Serves 8)

Mix in a glass or ceramic containter and let stand 10 minutes:
   2 cups TVP® chunks
   2 cups boiling water
   2 Tbsp. ketchup

Cover tightly and microwave on high for 5 minutes or simmer on the stove top for 10 minutes.

Combine in blender for the sauce:
   2 cloves garlic, crushed
   2 Tbsp. onion, chopped fine
   2 Tbsp. peanut butter
   2 Tbsp. tamari
   juice of half a lemon
   2 pieces of candied ginger, cut up
   1 tsp. coriander
   1/2 tsp. salt
   1/4 tsp. red pepper flakes

Whiz a few seconds in the blender. Place sauce in a 2 quart casserole, cover tightly, microwave on high 2 minutes. Combine chunks and sauce, cover tightly and microwave on medium power 7 minutes. Or bring sauce to a boil on top of the stove, add chunks, cover, reduce heat and simmer gently about 15 minutes until tender.

Per Serving: Calories: 76, Protein: 10 gm., Carbohydrates: 8 gm., Fat: 2 gm.

Kema

Pronounced key-ma, an East Indian feast dish.

Serves 6

Combine in a bowl and let stand 10 minutes:

1 cup TVP® granules
7/8 cup boiling water

Heat a large cast iron skillet or a wok and add:

1 Tbsp. olive oil
1 large yellow onion, minced
1 large garlic, crushed and minced
1" gingerroot, minced or grated

Stir fry about 5 minutes until onions are soft. Add the **TVP®** and stir fry 5 minutes.

Add and simmer a few minutes:

3 Tbsp. tomato paste
1 cup stewed tomatoes
2 to 3 tsp. curry power
1 tsp. salt
1/8 tsp. cayenne

Add:

1 cup fresh or frozen green peas
1 cup mushrooms, sliced

You can substitute a cup of green beans or carrots, cut into matchsticks, or a cup of corn. Bring the mixture to a boil, cover, and simmer over low heat 5 minutes. Serve at once on hot rice.

Per Serving: Calories: 118, Protein: 10 gm., Carbohydrates: 16 gm., Fat: 2 gm.

Curried Chunks and Vegetables

Curry sauce is better made a day ahead so the flavor has time to mellow.

Serves 6

Combine in a sauce pan:
1 cup TVP® chunks
1 cup hot water
1 Tbsp. ketchup

Let stand 5 minutes, then add 1 cup water and simmer 20-25 minutes until tender. Or add 1/4 cup water, cover tightly with plastic wrap, microwave on medium high power 8 to 10 minutes.

For the sauce, heat a pan and sauté until soft:
2 Tbsp. margarine or light sesame oil
1 medium onion, chopped

Sprinkle onion with:
3 Tbsp. flour
1-2 Tbsp. curry powder

Cook a few minutes, then stir in and cook until smooth and bubbly:
1 medium apple, peeled and chopped
2 cups vegetable broth or half broth, half coconut milk*

Taste sauce and add salt as needed. At this stage, sauce can be left in the refrigerator for a day or two. Add chunks to sauce, heat, and add hot vegetables before serving.

Peel and simmer in water to cover until tender:
2 carrots, cut in 1/2" chunks
1 small white turnip, sliced
1 small cauliflower, broken into flowerets

Drain vegetables, and combine with the curry sauce and cooked chunks. Serve over fluffy brown rice and accompany with small bowls of chopped green onions, chopped peanuts, coconut flakes, raisins and chutney to sprinkle on each serving as desired.

To make coconut milk pour **1 cup hot soymilk** over **1/2 cup coconut flakes** and let stand 2 hours. Strain.

Per Serving: Calories: 131, Protein: 8 gm., Carbohydrates: 19 gm., Fat: 2 gm.

Red Pepper Stir-Fry

Picutured on the cover, a favorite dish.

Serves 6-8

Mix and let stand 10 minutes:
   2 cups TVP® chunks
   2 cups hot water
   2 Tbsp. ketchup
   2 Tbsp. tamari

Cover tightly with plastic wrap and microwave on medium high power 10 minutes or until tender, or add 1 cup hot water and simmer top of stove about 20 minutes.

Prepare the vegetables:
   1 medium onion, sliced in thin wedges
   1 green pepper, in 1-inch sticks
   1 red pepper, in 1-inch sticks
   1 cup celery, sliced thinly on the diagonal
   1 cup mushrooms, sliced

Heat a large wok over medium high heat and add:
   2 Tbsp. dark sesame oil
   2 cloves garlic, minced
   1 Tbsp. raw ginger, chopped

Cook a minute, then add the onions, peppers, etc. to the hot oil and stir fry 5 to 10 minutes until crisp tender. Stir in the **TVP®** and add:
   1 cup vegetable broth
   1 Tbsp. tamari

Stir and cook until broth bubbles up. Serve with rice. Garnish with sliced green onions if desired.

Per Serving: Calories: 104, Protein: 10 gm., Carbohydrates: 11 gm., Fat: 4 gm.

Tangy Green Pepper Stir-Fry

With its oriental flavor, this is always a winner.

Serves 6

Soak for 5 minutes:
1 cup TVP® chunks
1 Tbsp. ketchup
1 cup hot water

Cover tightly and microwave on high for 8 minutes or add 1/2 cup liquid and simmer on top of stove 20 minutes until tender.

Mix for a marinade:
1/4 cup tamari
1/4 cup mirin (See Ingredients, page 7)
2 Tbsp. arrowroot or cornstarch
1 tsp. dark sesame oil
1 tsp. honey
1/2 cup vegetable stock

Let cooked chunks soak in marinade an hour or overnight.

Have ready:
1 1/2 cups onions, sliced in half moons
1 large green pepper (or 2 small), sliced

Heat a wok or skillet and add:
1 Tbsp. peanut oil
1 tsp. dark sesame oil

Sauté the onions and peppers 2-3 minutes, mix in the drained chunks and stir fry. Add to the remaining marinade:
1 cup vegetable broth

Add to pan and stir fry 1 minute. Serve on hot rice.

Per Serving: Calories: 164, Protein: 6 gm., Carbohydrates: 24 gm., Fat: 6 gm.

Oriental Chunks with Leeks

A subtle but marvelous combination of flavors.

Serves 8

Combine and let stand 20 minutes:

**1 cup TVP® chunks
2 cups boiling water
1 Tbsp. ketchup**

Cover and simmer about 20 minutes until tender. Or microwave on medium high power 8 to 10 minutes.

Meanwhile, cut off the root and most of the green tops from:

3 medium leeks

Wash them very carefully to get all the sand out. Slice 1/4" thick and drop into a quart of boiling salted water for 5 minutes. Drain immediately, keep warm.

Mix in a saucepan:

**1 1/2 cups vegetable broth
1/4 cup tamari
1 1/2 Tbsp. brown sugar
2 Tbsp. dark sesame oil
2 Tbsp. mirin** (See Ingredients, page 7) **or sherry
2 Tbsp. cornstarch**

Cook the sauce over medium low heat or in a microwave oven until it is thick and smooth, stirring occasionally. Add the drained cooked **TVP®** to the sauce, bring to a boil and pour over the warm leeks. Sauce and chunks are even better prepared the day before, then reheated and served over freshly cooked leeks.

Per Serving: Calories: 82, Protein: 4 gm., Carbohydrates: 10 gm., Fat: 4 gm.

Teriyaki Kabobs

*Children may prefer a pineapple chunk rather than onion on their kabobs. Sort out the largest **TVP®** chunks you can find for these.*

Serves 8

Combine and let stand for 30 minutes, then simmer until tender, 30 minutes, or cover tightly with plastic wrap and microwave on medium high power 10 to 12 minutes, adding a little water or vegetable broth as needed:

2 cups large TVP® chunks
2 cups hot water
2 Tbsp. ketchup

Chunks should be fork-tender, but not mushy. Drain chunks.

Combine for the marinade:

1 Tbsp. raw ginger, chopped
2 cloves garlic, minced
1 Tbsp. honey
1/4 cup tamari
1/4 cup mirin (See Ingredients, page 7) **or white wine**
1/2 cup vegetable broth (See Ingredients, page 8)

Add the cooked chunks to the marinade. Let soak 2 hours or longer. Soak 24 wooden skewers 30 minutes in water to prevent burning.

Thread chunks onto skewers, alternating with **cherry tomato halves, onion or pineapple squares, green pepper and zucchini slices.**

Broil on both sides over charcoal or under a preheated broiler, turn, brushing with leftover marinade.

Per Serving: Calories: 79, Protein: 8 gm., Carbohydrates: 15 gm., Fat: 0 gm.

Sweet and Sour TVP® with Pineapple

This is a tasty no-fat recipe that's simple to make.

Serves 6

Combine and let stand 5 minutes:
- **1 cup TVP® chunks**
- **1 Tbsp. ketchup**
- **1 1/4 cups hot water**

Cover tightly and microwave on medium high power 10 minutes or add 1/2 cup liquid and simmer in a covered pan until tender but not mushy (20-30 minutes).

Bring 1 cup water to a boil and add:
- **1 cup carrots (1 large carrot), sliced**
- **1 green pepper, cut in 1" squares**

Cover, return to boil and cook for 2 minutes to crisp-tender. Remove from heat, drain, reserving liquid. Return liquid to pan and add juice from:
- **1 (20 oz.) can unsweetened pineapple chunks**

Bring the liquid to a boil, adding:
- **1/4 cup sugar**
- **1/4 cup cider vinegar**

In a small bowl, combine:
- **2 Tbsp. cornstarch**
- **1/4 cup tamari**

Stir the cornstarch mixture into the hot liquid; the sauce will thicken and come to a boil almost at once. Add the cooked **TVP®**, the carrots, peppers, and pineapple to the sauce. Serve on rice or crisp chow mein noodles. This can be made ahead and reheated later.

Per Serving: Calories: 234, Protein: 6 gm., Carbohydrates: 56 gm., Fat: 0 gm.

Supplemental Recipes
Brown Rice

1 cup uncooked rice makes 3 to 3 1/2 cups cooked

This method of cooking insures that each grain will be separate and the rice will have a delicious nutty flavor. For every cup of brown rice use 2 cups liquid. Heat a 2-quart pan and add the rice. Cook and stir over medium high heat for 6 to 8 minutes, or until rice begins to pop. Remove from heat, add the hot water or vegetable stock, being careful of steam. Cover pan, return to heat, reduce heat to low and simmer 30-40 minutes until rice is tender and liquid is absorbed.

Per 3/4 Cup Serving: Calories: 135, Protein: 3 gm., Carbohydrates: 29 gm., Fat: 4 gm.

Homemade Tortillas or Chapatis

Makes 10

Mix together:
1 cup unbleached flour
1 cup whole wheat flour
1/2 tsp. salt

Mix and add slowly, just enough to make a soft dough:
1 tsp. oil
3/4 cup water

If dough is sticky, add a little more flour. Knead a few minutes, cover with a towel and let sit 20 minutes. Divide dough into 10 balls and roll each ball out into a thin circle about 10" in diameter. Keep dough and tortillas covered with a damp towel so they do not dry out. Most purchased tortillas are precooked; before filling, homemade ones should be cooked a little longer than the store bought ones on not quite as hot a griddle.

Per Tortilla: Calories: 84, Protein: 3 gm., Carbohydrates: 17 gm., Fat: 0 gm.

Dessert

Old Fashioned Mince Pie

My grandmother was famous for her mincemeat pies, which she made for the winter holidays using minced boiled beef. This pie is thick and rich in flavor, reminiscent of the my Grandmother's pies, but a much healthier recipe. The filling can be made a week ahead and refrigerated.

Serves 8-10

Place in a large kettle:

1 cup TVP® granules
1 cup hot water
4 cups tart apples, peeled and diced
1 cup raisins or currants (or half and half)
1/2 cup apple cider
1/2 cup brown sugar (If apples are not tart, reduce sugar)
grated rind and juice of 1 orange
grated rind and juice of 1 lemon

Bring mixture to a boil, reduce heat and simmer gently until apples are soft, about 20 minutes.

Stir in:

1 tsp. each cinnamon, nutmeg and mace
1/2 tsp. allspice
1/2 cup chopped walnuts (optional)

Cook 5 minutes more. Keep in a covered jar in refrigerator until ready to use. Makes 1 quart.

Have ready:

double crust for 9" pie

Line a 9" pie plate with the bottom crust, fill with mince mixture, top with crust, seal edges by crimping together, slash top in 6 places. Brush a little milk or soymilk onto crust. Bake at 375° about 1 hour until nicely browned. If pie begins to brown too soon, lay a piece of foil lightly over top.

Per Serving: Calories: 281, Protein: 7 gm., Carbohydrates: 46 gm., Fat: 10 gm.

Index

Where to Buy TVP®

For information on getting the three sizes of TVP® used in this cookbook, plus other textured soy and soy products, nutritional yeast and instant gluten flour, get a free catalog from:

The Mail Order Catalog
P.O. Box 180-TC
Summertown, TN 38483

1-800-695-2241
Order online: www.healthy-eating.com

Soyfoods for
the American
Table - $9.95

I Can't
Believe It's
Not Meat -
$9.95

Tofu &
Soyfoods
Cookery -
$12.95

Meatless
Burgers -
$9.95

The Magic
of Soy -
$9.95

Tofu Cookery - $15.95